Happy Birthday,

Mom and Dad
& Sisters
3 - 1991

Looking at COMPUTER
SOUNDS and MUSIC

BY PENNY HOLLAND

AN EASY-READ COMPUTER ACTIVITY BOOK

Franklin Watts

New York   London   Toronto   Sydney

1986

For Jim & Stacy

The author would like to thank her friend
Tom Thorpe for his sound advice.

Photographs courtesy of Insoft: p. 14; Intellivision: p. 16;
Kurzweil Computer Products: 23.

Library of Congress Cataloging in Publication Data

Holland, Penny.
Looking at computer sounds and music.

(An easy-read computer activity book)
Includes index.
Summary: An introduction to how computers make
music and synthesize sounds and speech, with
related projects.
1. Computer sound processing—Juvenile literature.
2. Computer music—Juvenile literature.
[1. Computer sound processing. 2. Computer
music] I. Title. II Series: Holland, Penny. Easy-read
computer activity book.
TK7895.S65H65 1986   006.5   85-22508
ISBN 0-531-10097-9

Contents

*Indicates an activity will be found on this page.

Imagine going to your friend's house. Your
friend's mom greets you at the door and says,
"Go on up!" As you climb the stairs, you hear
strange voices coming from the room. Does your
friend have other visitors? Suddenly the hall is
filled with the sounds of instruments tuning up.
Then they begin to play. You wonder if your friend
has invited over an entire marching band. But
when you enter the room there's only your
friend . . . and one very talented computer.

The Sounds Computers Make

Can *your* computer talk or play music? It can probably make some kinds of sounds. Listen carefully the next time you turn it on. You might hear a humming fan, the whirring disk drive, or a beep telling you that the computer is ready and waiting.

Two of these sounds are produced from moving mechanical parts. Only one is made electronically. Do you know which one it is? If you think the beep is electronic, you are right. That is the kind of computer sound this book is all about.

Of course computers can do more than beep. They can make clicks, buzzes, and musical tones. Put the correct musical notes together and your computer can play a tune. With special equipment attached to your computer, it can make some rather fancy music. In fact, it can even talk to you.

To understand how computers do these things, we first need to take a look at what makes sound.

How Sound Is Made

All sounds are caused by **vibrations** in the air. Tap on this book. When your finger hits the book, it causes a vibration that sends out sound waves. When a sound wave reaches your ear, it causes your eardrum to vibrate. That sends a signal to your brain, and you hear a tapping noise.

If you could look at a picture of a sound wave, it would tell you about the sound. A sound wave that makes many vibrations each second like this ᴧᴧᴧᴧ comes from a **high-pitched** sound, such as a shrill whistle, a tinkly bell, or the squeak of a mouse. A sound wave that makes only a few vibrations each second like this ⌒⌒ comes from a **low-pitched** sound, such as the beat of a drum, or the roar of a lion or a motorcycle. The number of vibrations per second is called the **frequency** of the sound.

Besides being high or low, sounds can also be loud or soft. A loud sound makes a tall sound wave like this ᴧᴧᴧ .

A soft sound has a short sound wave like this ⌒⌒⌒ .

Some Things to Do

ROAR, GROWL, SCREAM, AND SQUEAK: Use your voice to practice different sounds—high and low, loud and soft. For this activity you need some index cards and a pencil or marker. On one card draw a sound wave for a loud, high-pitched sound. It should look like this 〰 . On another card draw a sound wave for a soft, high-pitched sound. It should look something like this 〰 . Make two more cards, one for a loud, low-pitched sound like this 〰 and one for a soft, low-pitched sound like this 〰 . Shuffle the cards, draw one, and make your voice match the sound wave with a roar, growl, scream, or squeak.

SPEAK UP! You may also ROAR, GROWL, SCREAM AND SQUEAK with a friend. For this game you need sixteen index cards. Make four sets of the sound wave cards described above. Shuffle the cards and deal eight, face down, to each player. To play, you each turn over a card at the same time and make the sound. A loud sound wins over a soft sound and a high-pitched sound wins over one that is low-pitched. The person whose sound ''wins'' keeps both cards. If there is a tie, you each keep your own card. But watch out! If your friend catches you making an incorrect sound, then your friend gets your card. The game is over when one player has captured all the cards and the room is quiet. Whew!

How Does a Computer Make Sounds?

All sounds—even those of a computer—come from vibrations. Computer sounds are made by switching one of the computer's circuits ON and OFF.

This creates a small electrical **pulse** ⎍⎍⎍.

The pulse is sent through a device inside the computer called an **amplifier**. The amplifier makes

the pulse larger . This

larger pulse is then sent to the computer's **speaker**. Speakers are also found in radios, TVs, and stereos. When the speaker vibrates, you hear the sound.

Just as your voice can make high and low sounds, so can the computer. If its circuit switches on and off very fast, its pulse looks like this

and you hear a high sound. Slower on and off switching causes *less* frequent pulses like this

which make a low sound.

You can **program** your computer to make sounds. That means you can give it a set of instructions that will cause the computer to make sounds. The next activity gives examples of sound programs in BASIC—a language most computers understand.

Something to Try

BASIC SOUNDS: Here are some programs for making computer sounds. Because each kind of computer has its own special set of programming commands, you will need to choose the program listed for your brand of computer. If none of these programs works for your computer, perhaps you know somebody who can help you write one.

Turn the computer on and type your program on the keyboard. Press the RETURN or ENTER key at the end of each line. When you are finished, type **RUN** to run the program. Listen carefully for the sound. Be sure to ask for help if you've never done this sort of thing before.

APPLE II COMPUTERS:

```
 5 FOR N = 1 TO 100
10 SOUND = PEEK (−16336)
15 NEXT N
20 END
```

This program makes a low, buzzing sound.
The number −16336 is the memory address of the Apple's speaker.

ATARI COMPUTERS (Model 400/800):

```
 5 SOUND 0,121,10,15
10 FOR T=1 TO 100: NEXT T
15 SOUND 0,0,0,0
20 END
```

Line 5 turns the sound on.
A "delay loop" in line 10 makes the sound continue.
Line 15 turns the sound off.

COMMODORE 64 COMPUTERS:

```
 5 FOR M=54272 TO 54276: POKE M,O: NEXT M
10 POKE 54296,15
15 POKE 54273,28: POKE 54278,49
20 POKE 54276,17
25 FOR DR=1 TO 2000: NEXT DR
30 POKE 54276,16
```

This program is more complicated than the others because the Commodore gives you more choices for making sounds. When you run the program it plays an A note for a few seconds.

IBM COMPUTERS:

```
 5 SOUND 440,20
10 END
```

The 440 makes an A note.
The 20 causes the note to play for about one second.

TRS 80 COMPUTERS (Model IV):

```
 5 SOUND 4, 10
10 END
```

The numbers after SOUND tell the note and how long it plays. Note values range from 0 to 7; length of playing time, from 0 to 31.

Do you like challenges? If so, try to find out how to make the sound last longer. Can you and your helper figure out programs for making other sounds? In trying to program your own sounds, you soon will see just how complicated computer sounds can get.

The Makings of Music

Music is sound that is pleasing to our ears. Musical **notes** are made by sound waves that have a certain number of vibrations per second. For instance, musicians know that if something vibrates 440 times in one second, it will make the note we call **A**. Faster vibrating creates higher notes, and slower vibrating causes lower ones. By making a computer's speaker vibrate at the proper frequency, you can get it to play any note.

It takes more than notes to make music. Can you hum a **tune**? A tune is a series of notes—one note played after another. You must hum each note for the proper length of time to make the tune sound just right. This is called **rhythm**. Two or more notes sounding at the same time produce what we call **harmony**. Put together tune, rhythm, and harmony, and you have music.

Something to Do

BOTTLED MUSIC: Rinse out several empty soda pop bottles for this musical activity. Fill a bottle halfway with water. Put the bottle in front of your lips and blow to make a sound. Fill another bottle with less water and blow on it. How does this sound compare with the first? Fill a third bottle almost full and see what kind of sound it makes. How does the water level change the tone? Which one makes the fastest vibrations?

Now get one or more friends to help you make BOTTLED MUSIC. First try to make two bottles sound the same. Can you make three bottles sound the first three notes of "Three Blind Mice"? If you have plenty of bottles, experiment with water levels until you can play an entire tune on them. For a super challenge, put together notes, rhythm, and harmony, and try to play "Row, Row, Row Your Boat" in a round. (HINT: You may need as many as twelve bottles and *lots* of friends!)

Ready-Made Computer Sounds

Programming your computer to play even those simple tunes you tried in the bottle activity takes complicated computer programs. Most people just don't want to spend that much time on computer sounds. Yet many people *do* want their computers to make music. Fortunately there is an easier way. You can use **music software**—ready-made music programs for your computer.

Most music software comes on a disk and is ready to use on your computer. Once you start the program, making music is fun and easy. With some programs, you might use a **joystick**, a **graphics tablet**, or a **mouse** to help you make music. With others, you simply press the **keys** on the keyboard. Some programs are designed to teach you to read music, or to test your ability to tell one note from another. Other programs let you compose music that you can play back at the push of a button. With programs such as these, you can change notes easily and even print out a musical score on paper to share with your musical friends.

Something to Try

COMPUTERIZED MUSIC: Try out a ready-made music program on your computer. If you don't have one, go to a store that sells software, and ask for a demonstration. What kind of music can you make? Is the program easy to use? If not, how would you change it?

Synthesized Music

So far, we have been dealing with very simple computer music. You might have noticed its tinny and rather mechanical sound. It just can't measure up to your favorite rock group.

But computer music *can* get much fancier. It can sound like many different instruments—a whole orchestra, in fact. Of course this requires a much more complicated program and special equipment, such as better speakers and a music **synthesizer** connected to the computer.

Synthesize means to make something in a way other than the natural way. You probably have clothes made of synthetic materials such as polyester or nylon. Musical sounds of various instruments can be synthesized, too. To do this, the computer has to copy the sound a particular instrument makes. This means someone has to study the special sound wave patterns of that instrument and then get the computer to make a sound with a matching wave pattern. If it's done carefully, most people cannot tell the computer sound from the real thing.

Some Things to Do

EXPERIMENTING WITH SOUND: You can do some sound experiments with a friend. Collect some things that make similar sounds such as a bell, xylophone, whistle, and a glass of water. Blindfold your friend and make a sound with one of your items. Ask your friend to guess what made the sound. Can you tap a spoon on the glass of water and make it sound like the xylophone or the bell? What other things can you find that sound alike? Try to describe what makes a particular sound distinctive. If an organ and a piano played exactly the same tune, would you be able to tell them apart? Explain how their sounds are different.

THE "REAL" THING: Have you ever listened to synthesized music? Whether you realize it or not, you probably have. The music you hear as the background of many movies is synthesized. Go to the library or to a music store and get a record of synthesized music. Listen to it. What do you think? Does it sound different from real music? Can you find any synthesized music that you cannot tell from the real thing?

Computerized Sound Effects

Imagine this scene from a movie:

With the sound of horses galloping and guns shooting, the posse chases a band of outlaws out of town. Then a dog barks and a baby cries. Next, with its siren howling, a fire truck roars into town and screeches to a halt. Just then, a UFO lands to the sound of eerie music. Its doors crank open, a ramp crashes to the ground, and out marches an army of robots in clanking armor.

This imaginary movie seems more like a nightmare! But if anyone is crazy enough to want to make a movie like this, all the sound effects *could* be made by computers. Because movie producers have discovered that it often costs less to produce sounds by computers than to make the real sound, you have probably heard lots of computerized sound effects in movies. The *Star Wars* movies are examples of films that make good use of computerized sound effects.

Something to Do

NOISE-MAKERS: Before the days of television, people listened to their favorite radio programs. Actors spoke the words, and sound effects came from all sorts of things. Clapping half coconut shells on wood sounded like horses galloping. Rubbing sandpaper blocks together made the sound of rain on a window.

Try making up your own "noisy" story. Invite some friends to help. Collect items to use for sound effects. If you have a cassette recorder, tape your work. Play your tape or perform your story "live" for some friends. How do your sound effects compare with the ones you hear on TV or in the movies?

Talking Computers

Have you ever heard a computer talk? Before you say no, think carefully. Talking computers are becoming more common every day. There are talking cash registers in some grocery stores and cars that speak up to warn you that your door is ajar. Talking toys have been popular for years. Some teach young children sounds that animals make. Others say words for you to spell. Maybe you've even been helped by a talking computer when you dialed information for a telephone number.

These are all examples of talking computers that use **digitized** speech. That means a person's voice is recorded saying different words or sounds. When these sounds are changed into number codes, we say they are digitized. The codes are stored in a computer. Whenever you wish, the computer can turn the code back into sounds. Sometimes it can even ''speak'' the prerecorded words or sounds in many different combinations. This kind of talking computer sounds very natural. The only problem is that it takes a gigantic memory in order for it to say many words.

Something to Do

DIGITIZED ROBOT: Pretend you are a robot with a speech digitizer. How many different sentences that make sense can you make from combinations of these fifteen words stored in your program?

I	WENT	IS	THE	TREE
HE	RAN	IN	HIS	DOG
SHE	SANG	TO	MY	HOUSE

New, Improved, Talking Computers

The talking computers described above are fine for special uses. But wouldn't you rather have a computer that could say *any* word? Just think of the fun you could have with it! It could read you stories, play games with you, or maybe even tell you what ingredient to add next when you are making a batch of cookies.

Computers that talk make wonderful helpers to people with handicaps, too. Today many blind people know about the **Kurzweil machine**. It is a computer that can "look at" a printed page and read it aloud. A talking computer can also serve as a voice for someone who is unable to speak.

To do all of this talking, a computer needs to have an **unlimited vocabulary**. That means it must be able to say any word you give it. For this, you need a computer with a **speech synthesizer**.

What Is a Speech Synthesizer?

A speech synthesizer is a piece of computer equipment that copies the human voice. It is a small, integrated circuit that usually goes on a board inside the computer. The speech synthesizer works together with a special speech program on a disk.

Your job is to type the words for the computer to say. It won't start talking until you press the RETURN (or ENTER) key. The computer can also read a story or a letter you typed earlier and saved on a disk. It can even read aloud a message which comes to you over the telephone lines from another computer.

So far we've looked at *what* speech synthesizers can do. Now let's look at *how* they do it.

How Does a Speech Synthesizer Work?

A speech synthesizer says a word by going through the same steps many people do when they learn to read. First they learn the alphabet. Then they put letters together and sound them out.

Here's what happens. You type a word into your computer. The computer changes each key you press into a number code that it can "recognize" and work with. This is sort of like learning the alphabet.

Next comes the job of sounding-out. There are forty to fifty different sounds in the English language. These sounds are called **phonemes** (**FO**-NEEMS). If the computer can figure out which phoneme sounds are in a word, then it can pronounce the word. The computer's speech program does this. Using *hundreds* of rules, it turns the keyboard codes for a word into phoneme codes.

The last step is speaking the word. For this, the phoneme codes go to the computer's speech synthesizer which changes them into speech signals. The speech signals go through an amplifier, to the speaker. And lo and behold, the computer speaks.

Some Things to Do

HOW MANY SOUNDS?: Our English language is made up of twenty-six letters, but some letters have more than one sound. For each letter of the alphabet, try to think of how many different sounds it can make. Write a word that uses that sound. For instance, for the letter *A*, you might think of the sounds in the word FAR, FAT, and FATE. Can you think of any more *A* sounds? Do this for the whole alphabet. How many sounds did you find?

CODED SOUND: The sentences below have been written in a kind of code. See if you can figure it out. **KaN U RED THiS? THE KuMPUTR HaZ TU BE ABL TU MAK SeNS aND S@NDZ @T uV DiFRNT SiMBLZ. WheN iT DuZ iT KaN ToK.**

Did you figure it out? For our phoneme code, we used capital letters for the most common letter sounds, and also for long vowel sounds—the ones that say their own names. Small letters stand for short vowel sounds.

Continued on page 26

We needed some special symbols for sounds that are a combination of two letters, such as the @ for the **OU** sound in the word **out.** Use this idea, and try to make up your own phoneme code. Teach your code to a friend and try writing messages back and forth. Doing this will give you an idea of how computers have to translate words into code that will produce the correct sounds when spoken.

TRICKY WORDS: Most of the time, talking computers do a pretty good job of pronouncing the word that is typed. But they are not perfect. How do you think a computer would pronounce the word "**LEAD**?" If you read "YOU **LEAD** AND I'LL FOLLOW" or "**LEAD** IS A HEAVY METAL" you can see there are two ways to pronounce it. But they both look the same to the computer. Words like this are called **heteronyms (HET-**ER-O-**NYMs).**

How many tricky heteronyms can you think of that are spelled alike, but have different sounds and meanings? Make this into a game. List as many "tricky words" as you can think of in five minutes. Make sentences for each pair. Read the sentences aloud, substituting "tricky" for your special word. See if anyone can guess the pair of words you are thinking of.

Talking Back to Computers

Computers that understand everything we say are our dream for the future. Just think, instead of having to type instructions on your computer keyboard, you could *speak* your commands to the computer. While you are busy getting dressed in the morning, you could tell the computer a list of things you want to do during the day. While looking up information in a book, you could also be telling your computer what to write down.

A worker who needs both hands to do a job can speak out numbers for a computer to use in calculations. Computers that recognize speech are used for security systems, such as doors that un-lock at the sound of certain voices. Also people who have been injured and cannot use their hands to type can *speak* to their computers instead.

Today computers that recognize human speech are not very common. Most have a very limited vocabulary and are rather expensive. But that will change. Maybe in your lifetime you and all your friends will have computers that under-stand what you say. If you had one, how do you think you would use it?

Something to Do

BRAINSTORM: Get together with some friends and let your imagination go wild in a brainstorming session. Imagine having a fantastic computer that can speak and understand your speech. What all would you have it do? Think of the things you do each day and the many ways this computer could help you and your friends.

Computer Sounds in the Future

Right now computer sounds are just getting started. As you grow up watch how they grow and change, too. It's fun to look forward to the day when your computer will understand everything you say and will talk back—of course, only when you want it to. And just think how all thse fantastic computer sounds could affect TV, movies, and even video games!

Today, the scene at the beginning of this book is possible, but not very likely. In the future, perhaps we will all have computers that can speak with different voices and in many languages, too. When your friends come to visit they really *might* think you have a marching band in your bedroom—and an entire video arcade as well.

Finding Out More About Computer Sounds

READ COMPUTER MAGAZINES. Because computer sounds are rather new, you will probably find out more about them in magazines than in books. Ask your librarian or teacher what computer magazines are available.

> **3-2-1 CONTACT**, by Children's Television Workshop. Has a section entirely devoted to computer news, games, reviews, and programming.
> **FAMILY COMPUTING**, by Scholastic, Inc. Contains articles of interest to parents and children.
> **MICROZINE**, by Scholastic, Inc. A ''magazine'' on a disk. Several issues contain programs that let you make simple music on your computer.

CHOOSE THE BEST PROGRAMS. How do you decide which music program to buy for your computer? The best way is to read reviews of the latest software in computer magazines. Often magazines devote several pages to one subject, such as music. As you read, make a list of the programs that sound interesting. Write down everything you want *your* program to do. Do you want to be able to compose and play back music, print it out, or save your work?

Next call computer software stores. Tell them what equipment you have and what you are looking for. Ask for their recommendations. When you think you know what you want, go to the store and ask to *try* the program before buying it.

This same kind of careful shopping is helpful for buying any kind of program, whether it is a computer game, graphics software, or a speech synthesizer.

Words About Computer Sounds

Amplifier. A device that enlarges an electrical signal.

Digitize. To change into numbers, or into a numeric code.

Frequency. The number of vibrations made in one second.

Harmony. The sound of two or more notes playing together.

Heteronyms. Words that are spelled the same but have different pronounciations.

High-pitched sound. A sound caused by many vibrations per second.

Kurzweil machine. A special machine for the blind. It can read any printed page out loud.

Low-pitched sound. A sound caused by only a few vibrations per second.

Music synthesizer. A computerized copy of musical sounds.

Note. A musical tone created by a certain frequency.

Phonemes. The different sounds that make up our speech.

Rhythm. The speed or timing used in music.

Sound wave. Pressure waves carrying a sound through the air.

Speaker. A device that changes electrical signals into sound vibrations you can hear.

Speech recognition. A computer's ability to recognize human speech and change it to printed words.

Speech synthesizer. The hardware and software that enables a computer to talk.

Vibrations. Rapid back and forth movements that are the source of all sounds.

Index